W9-CHO-983

when i am not myself

KATHY DeZARN BEYNETTE

Pomegranate **kids**®

Published by PomegranateKids®, an imprint of
Pomegranate Communications, Inc.
19018 NE Portal Way, Portland OR 97230
800 227 1428 | www.pomegranate.com

Pomegranate Europe Ltd.
Unit 1, Heathcote Business Centre, Hurlbutt Road
Warwick, Warwickshire CV34 6TD, UK
[+44] 0 1926 430111 | sales@pomeurope.co.uk

To learn about new releases and special offers from Pomegranate, please
visit www.pomegranate.com and sign up for our e-mail newsletter.
For all other queries, see "Contact Us" on our home page.

© 2014 Kathy DeZarn Beynette

The contents of this book are protected by copyright, including all images and
all text. This copyrighted material may not be reproduced or transmitted in
any form or by any means, electronic or mechanical, including but not limited
to photocopying, scanning, recording, or by any information storage or
retrieval system, without the express permission in writing of the copyright
holders. All rights to the images and text are reserved.

This product is in compliance with the Consumer Product Safety Improve-
ment Act of 2008 (CPSIA) and any subsequent amendments thereto. A
General Conformity Certificate concerning Pomegranate's compliance with
the CPSIA is available on our website at www.pomegranate.com, or by request
at 800 227 1428. For additional CPSIA-required tracking details, contact
Pomegranate at 800 227 1428.

Library of Congress Control Number: 2013943832

ISBN 978-0-7649-6673-6

Pomegranate Catalog No. A230
Designed by Carey Hall

Printed in China
23 22 21 20 19 18 17 16 15 14   10 9 8 7 6 5 4 3 2 1

For
Camille
and
Calvin

When I am a Zebra
My stripes look OK,
But I'd like to try
Wearing checks for one day.

When I am a **Rabbit**
I get very quiet.
I act really shy;
You might want to try it.

When I am a Bear
I patiently wait
For the day my brother
Will go hibernate.

When I am a **Gator**
Just tell me, "Good night."
Don't say, "See you later."
That line's become trite.

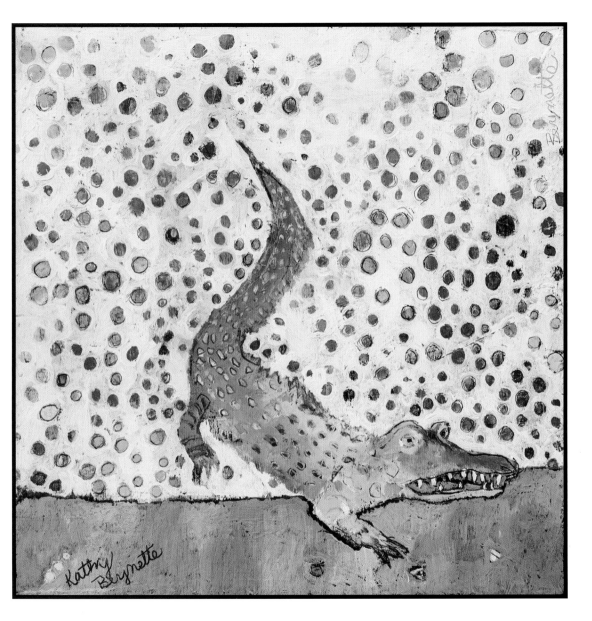

When I'm a giraffe
My food's high on a shelf;
I put it up there
to share just with myself.

When I'm a **Giraffe**
My food's high on a shelf;
I put it up there
To share just with myself.

When I am a Lion
I need to be free;
The circus is not
The best place for me.

When I am a Rat
Folks offer me cheese
On weird little plates
That SNAP, pinch, and squeeze!

When I am a **Poodle**
I go to the groomer;
My collar's not diamonds—
That's just an old rumor.

When I am a Ram,
It would be better
If you don't knit me
a turtleneck sweater.

When I am a **Ram**
I think it'd be better
If you wouldn't knit me
A turtleneck sweater.

When I am a **Kitten**
I wait in a row
For someone to love,
For someplace to go.

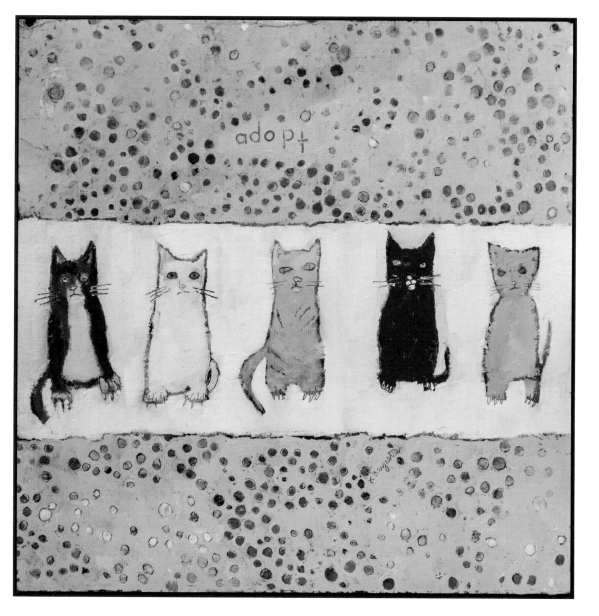

When I am a Trout
I'm on a swim team;
We beat all the other
Fish in the stream!

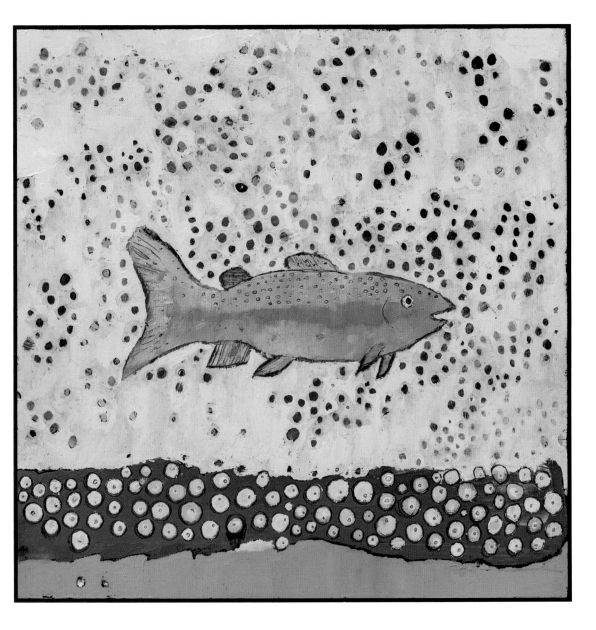

When I am a Shrimp
I already know
That I'm very tiny
So don't tell me so.

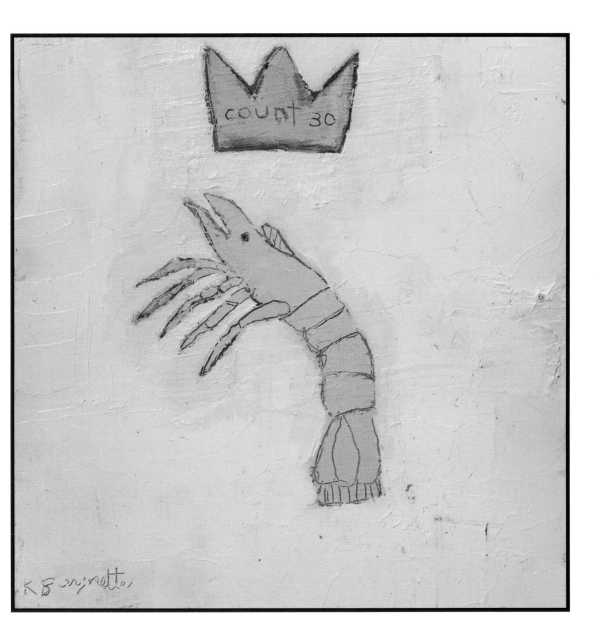

When I'm an **Anteater**
Just guess what I eat!
I put sugar on them
To make them taste sweet.

When I'm a Raccoon
And masked like a bandit,
I steal food from your trash—
Rotten egg? I can stand it!

When I'm a Raccoon
And masked like a bandit,
I eat from your trash—
Rotten egg? I can stand it!

When I am a **Turtle**
And I know you well,
I don't have to spend
Much time in my shell.

Kathy Beynette

When I am a **Hound**
I'm close to the ground;
That's where the most treats
Are usually found.

When I am a Turkey
And it is November,
I dress up like someone
You will not remember.

When I am a Turkey
And it is November
I dress up like someone
You will not remember.

Kathy Bergnette

When I am a Wolf
I don't think it's good
That I'm the bad guy
In *Red Riding Hood*.

When I am an **Owl**
It's truly all right
With my mom or dad
If I'm out all night.

When I'm a polar bear
I would rather be cold
than move to Miami
When I get old.

When I'm a **Polar Bear**
I'd rather be cold
Than move to Miami
When I'm getting old.

When I am a Crow
I take shiny things:
Holiday tinsel
And lost diamond rings;
Mirrors and tin foil
And dragonfly wings.

When I'm a Kangaroo
My pouch is for baby;
She's there all the time.
Is it too much? Maybe.

When I am **Myself**
(as I have been since birth),
I'm a little bit like
Most creatures on Earth.

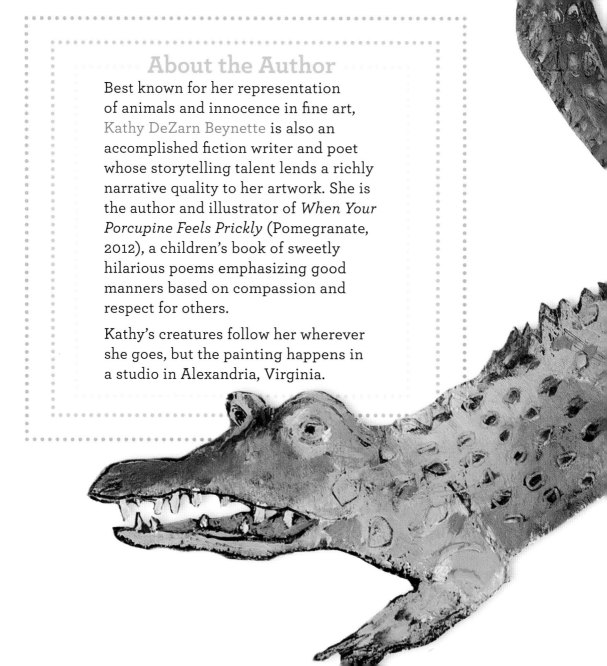

About the Author

Best known for her representation of animals and innocence in fine art, Kathy DeZarn Beynette is also an accomplished fiction writer and poet whose storytelling talent lends a richly narrative quality to her artwork. She is the author and illustrator of *When Your Porcupine Feels Prickly* (Pomegranate, 2012), a children's book of sweetly hilarious poems emphasizing good manners based on compassion and respect for others.

Kathy's creatures follow her wherever she goes, but the painting happens in a studio in Alexandria, Virginia.